Raindrops
Roll

April Pulley Sayre

Beach Lane Books

New York   London   Toronto   Sydney   New Delhi

Rain is coming.
You can feel it
in the air.

The sky darkens with storm.

Insects take cover.

A firefly below a leaf.

A fly inside a pod.

Rain plops.
It drops.

It patters.

It spatters.

Rain waters...

and washes . . .

and weighs down.

It thuds.

Makes mud.

It fills.

It spills.

Rain stops.

They glob together.

Raindrop spangles
mark angles.

They cling to curves

and cover cocoons.

Raindrops settle.

They slip.

They dot.

They drip.

They magnify

and mingle

and moisten.

Raindrops reflect.

They reveal.

Raindrops highlight
what is real.

They linger in lines.

And when the sun shines . . .

raindrops

slowly

dry.

A SPLASH OF SCIENCE

Water has three forms: solid, liquid, and gas. Snow and ice are water in solid form. Rain, mist, and most fogs are water in liquid form. Water vapor, the gas, floats in the air. It is so tiny we cannot see it.

Rain Is Coming

Clouds are made of water vapor, water droplets, ice crystals, and a dash of dust. A cloud's water droplets and ice crystals scatter light, giving clouds their white or gray tint. The tiny water droplets in a cloud must come together to form bigger, heavier drops before they'll fall as rain. Dust helps this happen.

Dust acts as a nucleus. (Ice particles and microbes can also act as nuclei.) Water vapor cools and condenses on the dust nucleus. Tiny water droplets attach, making the drop bigger. But it's cold up in the air where clouds form. So the dust-and-water blob usually freezes almost instantly. It becomes an ice crystal. More ice crystals may attach, growing the "arms" that make a snowflake.

Snowflakes or ice crystals may fall from the cloud and reach the ground still frozen. Or, as they fall, they may warm and melt to become raindrops. Raindrops, even in summer, typically start as snow or ice high up in the clouds.

Rain Patters. It Spatters.

As raindrops fall, they may bump into one another and form bigger drops, or they may thin and break apart. Raindrops vary in size from about .5 millimeters to 4 millimeters.

Raindrops Dot

Raindrops aren't really the tear shape shown in cartoons and diagrams. Water molecules are attracted to one another. They cling together to make a sphere shape—the most closely packed shape they can form. The sphere flattens on the bottom as it falls through the air. A large drop may also be flattened where it rests on a flat surface such as a leaf.

Raindrops Cling

Water wets many surfaces. It spreads out and soaks in. But some leaf surfaces are waxy and repel water. On these, raindrops settle as blobs.

In the world of beetles and roly-polies and ants, water can be downright sticky. A water droplet can stick to a butterfly's antennae. It can be very hard for a small insect to shake off a big drop of water. Yet these creatures also need water. An ant may stop to take a drink by sticking its mouth into a raindrop as big as its head!

Raindrops Magnify

Think about eyeglasses, a camera lens, or a magnifying glass. They all have curved surfaces. They are all clear. Light passes through them. A raindrop has these qualities too. Its inner and outer surfaces bounce, bend, and transmit light, making whatever's beneath it appear larger.

Raindrops Reflect

In some of this book's photos you can see reflections of a tree, a leaf, a flower, or the camera's flashes. The surfaces of a raindrop can reflect light the way a mirror does. They bounce light back toward the viewer. Look at a raindrop and you may even see yourself.

Raindrops Fill and Spill

Raindrops travel. They are part of a vast system called the water cycle. Some raindrops drip off plants and animals and flow downhill into creeks, then rivers, then the ocean.

Raindrops Dry

Raindrops also go through a process called evaporation. The sun heats the water in a puddle or on a leaf. That heat helps the water turn from liquid into gas: water vapor. The invisible water vapor rises up from the puddle or leaf into the sky to form clouds. Then it may become raindrops once again.

Raindrops Inside You

Earth's water is always being naturally recycled and reused. Raindrops that drip off trees and roll into rivers end up in glasses of water you drink. Rainwater from long ago is pumped from underground rivers and into faucets and sinks.

Plants pull rainwater from the soil. The water plumps tomatoes and apples as they grow. So you don't just drink former raindrops, you eat them too!

You return raindrops to the sky. Your breath is moist and full of water. The water you breathe out may become part of a cloud. It may fall as rain on a mountain, far away. When your tears dry, the water vapor goes into the air and could someday rain down again too.

To splash around in more water science, visit AprilSayre.com
and dip into the resources listed below.

Kerley, Barbara. *A Cool Drink of Water.* Washington, DC: National Geographic Children's Books, 2006.

Martin, Jacqueline Briggs. *Snowflake Bentley.* Boston: Houghton Mifflin, 1998.

Wick, Walter. *A Drop of Water.* New York: Scholastic, 1997.

Community Collaborative Rain, Hail, and Snow Network: cocorahs.org

United States Geological Survey Water Science School: water.usgs.gov/edu

For Andrea Welch, who loves the rain

THANK YOU to Barb Crighton and her husband, John, for allowing me to photograph their garden on a moment's notice every time it rained. Thank you to my husband, Jeff Sayre, for finding and photographing the tree frog peeking out of our cup plants. (Thanks also for welcoming a certain rain-soggy wife back into the house again and again!) I appreciate the contributions of Lauren Rille, designer extraordinaire.

Thank you to the following experts, who helped review the end matter for this book: physicist Dr. Les Cowley of Atmospheric Optics (atoptics.co.uk); Sam Lashley, senior meteorologist, National Weather Service, Northern Indiana Office; Mike Hoffman, chief meteorologist for WNDU-TV and Ag Day/US Farm Report meteorologist; and climatologist Dr. Steven Quiring, associate professor, Texas A&M.

BEACH LANE BOOKS An imprint of Simon & Schuster Children's Publishing Division • 1230 Avenue of the Americas, New York, New York 10020 • Copyright © 2015 by April Pulley Sayre • All rights reserved, including the right of reproduction in whole or in part in any form. • BEACH LANE BOOKS is a trademark of Simon & Schuster, Inc. • For information about special discounts for bulk purchases, please contact Simon & Schuster Special Sales at 1-866-506-1949 or business@simonandschuster.com. • The Simon & Schuster Speakers Bureau can bring authors to your live event. For more information or to book an event, contact the Simon & Schuster Speakers Bureau at 1-866-248-3049 or visit our website at www.simonspeakers.com. • Book design by Lauren Rille • The text for this book is set in Quickrest and Bodoni. • Manufactured in China • 1023 SCP • 10 9 8 • Library of Congress Cataloging-in-Publication Data • Sayre, April Pulley, author. • Raindrops roll / April Pulley Sayre.—First edition. • p. cm. • Summary: "In her latest gorgeously photo-illustrated nonfiction picture book, celebrated author April Pulley Sayre sheds new light on the wonders of rain, from the beauty of a raindrop balanced on a leaf to the amazing, never-ending water cycle that keeps our planet in perfect ecological balance."— Provided by publisher. • Audience: Ages 4–8. • Audience: K to grade 3. • ISBN 978-1-4814-2064-8 (hardcover) • ISBN 978-1-4814-2065-5 (eBook) • 1. Hydrologic cycle—Juvenile literature. 2. Rain and rainfall—Juvenile literature. [1. Water.] I. Title. • GB848.S28 2015 • 551.48—dc23 • 2014018995